THE MINDFUL ENTREPRENEUR

Mastering Self-Discovery for Business Success

Patrick Odega

Dedication:

To all the mindful entrepreneurs who dare to embark on a journey of self-discovery and business success. May this book serve as a guiding light, illuminating the path to a harmonious and purposeful entrepreneurial life. Your dedication, resilience, and commitment to mindfulness inspire us all to create businesses that not only thrive but also nurture our well-being and make a positive impact on the world.

Table of Contents:

Chapter 1: Introduction

In recent years, entrepreneurship has experienced a remarkable surge in popularity and influence, transforming the global business landscape. In today's fast-paced and interconnected world, the traditional notions of employment and career paths are being redefined, inspiring individuals to take charge of their professional lives and embark on entrepreneurial endeavors.

One of the primary reasons for the rise of entrepreneurship is the desire for freedom and autonomy. Many individuals are no longer satisfied with the conventional nine-to-five work structure or the limitations of hierarchical organizations. They yearn for the flexibility to shape their own destinies, to follow their passions, and to have a meaningful impact on the world around them.

Moreover, the advancements in technology and the digital age have significantly lowered the barriers to entry for aspiring entrepreneurs. Access to information, resources, and global networks has never been more abundant. This has created unprecedented opportunities for individuals to turn their ideas into reality, build scalable businesses, and reach a global audience.

The shift in societal values has also played a significant role in the rise of entrepreneurship. People are increasingly prioritizing fulfillment, purpose, and personal growth over solely financial gains. Entrepreneurship provides a platform for individuals to align their work with their values, to pursue ventures that are meaningful to them, and to create a positive impact on their communities and the world.

Furthermore, the uncertain and rapidly changing economic landscape has made entrepreneurship an attractive option for many. Traditional job security has become increasingly elusive, and individuals are seeking alternative paths that offer greater resilience and adaptability. Entrepreneurship allows individuals to be proactive in shaping their future, leveraging their skills, and creating multiple income streams.

The rise of entrepreneurship in the modern world reflects a fundamental shift in the way people perceive work, success, and fulfillment. It represents a movement towards empowerment, self-expression, and the pursuit of one's passions. As more and more individuals recognize the potential and benefits of entrepreneurship, the entrepreneurial spirit continues to grow, driving innovation, economic growth, and personal fulfillment in our society.

The Importance of Mindfulness in Entrepreneurial Success

Entrepreneurship is a challenging and demanding journey filled with uncertainty, risks, and countless obstacles. In such a dynamic and ever-changing environment, the practice of mindfulness becomes a vital tool for entrepreneurs seeking sustainable success and well-being.

At its core, mindfulness is the practice of being fully present and engaged in the present moment, with a non-judgmental and accepting attitude. By incorporating mindfulness into their entrepreneurial journey, individuals can develop a heightened sense of self-awareness, which is essential for understanding their strengths, weaknesses, and triggers. This self-awareness allows entrepreneurs to harness their unique qualities and leverage them to their advantage while recognizing areas for growth and improvement.

In the face of constant challenges and setbacks, mindfulness empowers entrepreneurs to maintain a calm and clear mind. By cultivating an ability to observe their thoughts and emotions without being swept away by them, entrepreneurs can navigate obstacles with a sense of clarity and composure. This mental resilience allows them to stay focused on their goals, make rational decisions, and persevere through adversity.

Mindfulness also provides entrepreneurs with a valuable tool for managing stress and overwhelm. The entrepreneurial journey often entails long hours, high-pressure situations, and an immense amount of responsibility. By practicing mindfulness, entrepreneurs can develop the ability to recognize and respond to stress in a healthy and constructive manner.

They can learn to manage their energy, establish healthy boundaries, and prioritize self-care, ensuring that they maintain their well-being and avoid burnout.

Moreover, mindfulness enhances the ability to make wise and informed decisions. By cultivating a non-reactive and non-judgmental mindset, entrepreneurs can approach challenges with curiosity and open-mindedness. They can embrace a beginner's mindset, allowing them to see opportunities where others may only see obstacles. Through mindfulness, entrepreneurs develop the capacity to step back, assess situations objectively, and make decisions that are aligned with their values and long-term vision.

In the fast-paced world of entrepreneurship, it's easy to get caught up in the never-ending to-do lists, deadlines, and external pressures. Mindfulness brings entrepreneurs back to the present moment, reminding them to appreciate the journey and find joy in the process. By staying present and mindful, entrepreneurs can fully immerse themselves in their work, fostering creativity, innovation, and a deeper connection with their passion.

Practice of mindfulness serves as a powerful anchor for entrepreneurs amidst the chaos and uncertainties of the entrepreneurial journey. It enables them to cultivate self-awareness, maintain clarity and resilience, manage stress effectively, make wise decisions, and find fulfillment along the way. By integrating mindfulness into their entrepreneurial endeavors, individuals can unlock their full potential and create a sustainable path to success, both in business and in life.

Overview of the Book's Purpose and Structure

"The Mindful Entrepreneur" is more than just a book; it is a roadmap that empowers entrepreneurs to integrate mindfulness into their entrepreneurial journey and unlock their full potential. Through a comprehensive and structured approach, this book aims to provide practical insights, tools, and exercises that will guide readers in cultivating a mindful entrepreneurial mindset and achieving sustainable success.

The book begins by introducing the concept of mindfulness and its relevance in the entrepreneurial context. It highlights the transformative power of mindfulness and how it can enhance various aspects of an entrepreneur's life and business. By understanding the foundational principles of mindfulness, readers can grasp the importance of integrating it into their entrepreneurial endeavors.

The subsequent chapters delve into the key areas where mindfulness can have a significant impact on entrepreneurial success. The book explores the development of a mindful entrepreneurial mindset, emphasizing the cultivation of self-awareness, resilience, and a growth-oriented approach. It provides practical techniques and exercises to enhance self-reflection, manage stress, and maintain a balanced perspective amidst the challenges and uncertainties of entrepreneurship.

Building authentic connections and relationships is essential for entrepreneurial success, and this book recognizes the significance of mindfulness in this aspect. It guides readers on how to communicate mindfully, actively listen, and build strong connections based on empathy and understanding. It also explores conflict resolution and maintaining healthy partnerships through a mindful approach.

Furthermore, the book highlights the role of mindfulness in decision-making and problem-solving. It offers strategies for making conscious decisions, overcoming biases, and approaching problems with clarity and creativity. Readers will learn how to harness mindfulness to adapt to changing circumstances and make informed choices aligned with their values and long-term vision.

The book also addresses the importance of mindful leadership and ethical entrepreneurship. It explores mindful leadership principles and practices, emphasizing the integration of success and well-being. Readers will gain insights into creating a positive work culture, promoting social responsibility, and leading with integrity.

Throughout the book, readers will find practical exercises, meditations, and reflection prompts that they can integrate into their daily lives and entrepreneurial practices. Real-life examples and case studies illustrate how mindfulness can be applied in different entrepreneurial contexts, making the concepts tangible and relatable.

In the final chapters, the book provides resources for continued growth and personal development. It offers guidance on building a mindfulness practice that suits individual preferences and lifestyles. Readers will find recommendations for further reading, additional courses or workshops, and online resources to support their ongoing journey of mindfulness and entrepreneurship.

Overall, "The Mindful Entrepreneur" is a comprehensive guide that combines practical wisdom, research-based insights, and experiential exercises to empower entrepreneurs to navigate their journey with grace, purpose, and fulfillment. By integrating mindfulness into their entrepreneurial endeavors, readers can cultivate a mindful entrepreneurial mindset, make conscious decisions, build authentic relationships, and lead with integrity, ultimately achieving sustainable success in business and personal life.

Chapter 2:

Understanding Mindfulness

Mindfulness is a practice rooted in ancient Eastern traditions, particularly Buddhism, that has gained widespread recognition and adoption in modern society. At its essence, mindfulness involves cultivating a deliberate and non-judgmental awareness of the present moment, including one's thoughts, emotions, bodily sensations, and the surrounding environment. It is about intentionally paying attention to one's experience without getting caught up in judgment or attachment.

The core principles of mindfulness form the foundation upon which the practice is built. These principles guide individuals in developing a mindset and approach that can deepen their capacity for mindfulness. Here are some key principles:

1. Non-judgment: Mindfulness invites a stance of non-judgmental awareness. Rather than labeling experiences as

good or bad, right or wrong, mindfulness encourages individuals to observe their thoughts, emotions, and sensations without passing judgment. This non-judgmental attitude fosters self-acceptance, openness, and a deeper understanding of one's inner landscape.

2. Acceptance: Mindfulness emphasizes accepting the present moment as it is, without attempting to change or resist it. It involves acknowledging and embracing the full range of experiences, whether they are pleasant, unpleasant, or neutral. Acceptance allows individuals to develop a compassionate and non-reactive relationship with their experiences, promoting a sense of inner peace and well-being.

3. Present-moment focus: Mindfulness directs attention to the present moment experience. It encourages individuals to anchor their awareness in the here and now, rather than dwelling on the past or anticipating the future. By staying present, individuals can fully engage with their current tasks, relationships,

and surroundings, fostering a deep sense of presence and connection.

4. Non-striving: Mindfulness invites individuals to let go of the incessant need for achievement, striving, and goal-oriented thinking. It encourages a shift from constantly seeking outcomes and results to embracing the process and journey. Non-striving allows individuals to cultivate a sense of contentment and gratitude for the present moment, rather than constantly chasing future desires or dwelling on past regrets.

5. Beginner's mind: Mindfulness invites individuals to approach each moment with a sense of curiosity and openness, as if experiencing it for the first time. This "beginner's mind" attitude involves letting go of preconceived notions, assumptions, and expectations. By adopting a fresh perspective, individuals can cultivate a sense of wonder, explore new possibilities, and engage with their experiences with a sense of freshness and vitality.

6. Compassion: Compassion is an integral aspect of mindfulness. It involves

cultivating a kind and gentle attitude towards oneself and others. Mindfulness encourages individuals to treat themselves with understanding and empathy, embracing imperfections and offering self-care. Moreover, it fosters a sense of empathy and compassion towards others, nurturing harmonious relationships and a greater sense of interconnectedness.

By embracing these core principles, individuals can deepen their practice of mindfulness and apply it to various aspects of their lives, including entrepreneurship. These principles provide a framework for developing a mindset of presence, acceptance, and self-compassion, enabling entrepreneurs to navigate challenges, make conscious decisions, and cultivate a sense of fulfillment and well-being.

Benefits of Incorporating Mindfulness in Entrepreneurship

Incorporating mindfulness into entrepreneurship offers a wide range of benefits that can positively impact both personal well-being and business success. Here are some key benefits:

1. Enhanced Focus and Productivity: Mindfulness practices, such as meditation and deep breathing exercises, can improve focus and concentration. By training the mind to stay present, entrepreneurs can reduce distractions and enhance their ability to stay engaged in tasks. This increased focus leads to improved productivity and the ability to accomplish more in less time.

2. Stress Reduction and Resilience: Entrepreneurship can be stressful and demanding, but mindfulness provides effective tools for managing stress. Regular mindfulness practice helps individuals develop resilience and cope with the pressures of running a business. By cultivating a non-reactive and non-judgmental mindset, entrepreneurs can respond to challenges with clarity and composure, reducing the negative impact of stress on their mental and physical well-being.

3. Better Decision-Making: Mindfulness cultivates self-awareness, which is crucial for making informed and effective decisions. By being present in the moment and attuned to their thoughts, emotions, and intuition, entrepreneurs can make decisions that align with their values, long-term vision, and the needs of their business. Mindfulness helps individuals overcome biases, see situations from multiple perspectives, and make choices that are grounded in wisdom and clarity.

4. Increased Creativity and Innovation: Mindfulness practices foster a state of open awareness and non-judgment, which nurtures creativity and innovation. By stepping back from habitual thinking patterns and embracing a beginner's mind, entrepreneurs can approach problems with fresh perspectives and uncover innovative solutions. Mindfulness encourages thinking outside the box, promoting creative problem-solving and the ability to adapt to changing circumstances.

5. Improved Emotional Intelligence and Relationships: Mindfulness enhances emotional intelligence, which is essential for building authentic connections and maintaining healthy relationships in business.

By cultivating self-awareness and empathy, entrepreneurs can better understand and manage their own emotions and respond empathetically to the emotions of others. This leads to more effective communication, conflict resolution, and the establishment of positive work environments.

Dispelling Common Misconceptions about Mindfulness

Despite its growing popularity, mindfulness can be surrounded by misconceptions that prevent individuals from fully embracing its benefits. Here are a few common misconceptions about mindfulness that can be dispelled:

1. Mindfulness is about emptying the mind: Mindfulness does not aim to empty the mind or stop thoughts altogether. Rather, it involves observing

thoughts and allowing them to come and go without getting attached to or carried away by them. It's about developing a non-reactive and non-judgmental relationship with one's thoughts and experiences.

2. Mindfulness is time-consuming: Incorporating mindfulness into daily life doesn't necessarily require significant time commitments. Even short, regular mindfulness practices can have a meaningful impact. A few minutes of mindful breathing, a mindful walk, or a brief meditation session can help individuals cultivate presence and reap the benefits of mindfulness.

3. Mindfulness is solely about relaxation: While mindfulness can promote relaxation and stress reduction, it encompasses much more than that. Mindfulness is about being fully present and engaged with the reality of the moment, whether it's pleasant, neutral, or challenging. It involves embracing the full range of experiences and developing a balanced relationship with them.

4. Mindfulness is only for spiritual or religious individuals: Mindfulness is rooted in ancient spiritual traditions, but its practice has been secularized and made accessible to individuals from all backgrounds and belief systems. It can be embraced by anyone interested in improving their well-being, focus, and effectiveness, regardless of their religious or spiritual affiliations.

By understanding the true essence of mindfulness and dispelling these misconceptions, individuals can approach mindfulness with an open mind and fully harness its benefits in the entrepreneurial context

Chapter 3:

The Mindful Entrepreneurial Mindset

The mindset of an entrepreneur plays a crucial role in determining their success and overall well-being. A mindful entrepreneurial mindset encompasses several key elements that contribute to personal growth, resilience, and business success.

1. Developing Self-Awareness and Self-Reflection: Mindfulness begins with self-awareness, the ability to observe one's thoughts, emotions, and patterns of behavior without judgment. By developing self-awareness, entrepreneurs gain valuable insights into their strengths, weaknesses, and triggers. This self-reflection allows them to identify areas for growth and improvement, make conscious choices, and align their actions with their values and goals.

2. Cultivating a Growth Mindset and Embracing Challenges: A growth mindset is the belief that abilities and intelligence can be developed through dedication, effort, and a willingness to learn. Mindful entrepreneurs embrace challenges as opportunities for growth and see setbacks as valuable learning experiences. By adopting a growth mindset, entrepreneurs approach challenges with curiosity, perseverance, and a willingness to step out of their comfort zones. They view failures as stepping stones to success and remain open to feedback and continuous improvement.

3. Managing Stress, Uncertainty, and Setbacks through Mindfulness: Entrepreneurship is inherently filled with stress, uncertainty, and setbacks. Mindfulness equips entrepreneurs with tools to effectively manage these challenges. By practicing mindfulness techniques such as deep breathing, meditation, and body scan exercises, entrepreneurs can calm their minds, reduce stress, and enhance their ability to respond to difficult situations with clarity and composure. Mindfulness helps entrepreneurs develop resilience, bounce back from setbacks,

and maintain a sense of balance and well-being amidst the ups and downs of the entrepreneurial journey.

4. Enhancing Creativity and Innovation through Mindfulness: Mindfulness practices foster a state of open awareness, enabling entrepreneurs to tap into their creative potential. By quieting the mind and letting go of preconceived notions, entrepreneurs create space for new ideas and perspectives to emerge. Mindfulness encourages entrepreneurs to approach problems with fresh eyes, explore different possibilities, and think outside the box. By integrating mindfulness into their creative process, entrepreneurs can enhance innovation, make unique connections, and develop novel solutions to complex challenges.

By cultivating a mindful entrepreneurial mindset, entrepreneurs can develop self-awareness, embrace challenges, effectively manage stress and setbacks, and tap into their creative potential. This mindset empowers entrepreneurs to navigate the entrepreneurial journey with greater clarity, resilience, and a sense of purpose, ultimately leading to greater fulfillment and success in their business endeavors.

Chapter 4:
Building Mindful Relationships in Business

Building meaningful and mindful relationships is indeed crucial for success in the entrepreneurial world. Entrepreneurs who prioritize and incorporate mindfulness into their approach to relationships can create a positive and supportive business environment that fosters authentic connections, effective communication, and healthy collaborations. Here are some key elements for building mindful relationships in business:

1. Authenticity and Genuine Connection: Mindful entrepreneurs understand the importance of showing up authentically in their interactions with others. They strive to be true to themselves, transparent, and sincere in their communication. By being genuine and authentic, entrepreneurs create a sense of trust and credibility, fostering

stronger and more meaningful connections with their stakeholders.

2. Presence and Active Engagement: Mindful entrepreneurs bring a sense of presence and active engagement to their interactions. They are fully present in conversations, meetings, and collaborations, actively listening to others and valuing their perspectives. By giving their full attention and being genuinely interested in others' thoughts and ideas, entrepreneurs build rapport and create a sense of mutual respect.

3. Empathy and Understanding: Cultivating empathy is a fundamental aspect of building mindful relationships. Mindful entrepreneurs strive to understand the experiences, needs, and challenges of their stakeholders. They put themselves in others' shoes, seeking to grasp their perspectives and respond with empathy and compassion. By showing understanding and validating others' feelings, entrepreneurs foster a supportive and inclusive business environment.

4. Effective Communication: Mindful entrepreneurs recognize that effective communication is the cornerstone of successful relationships. They strive to communicate clearly, openly, and respectfully. Mindful entrepreneurs are mindful of their words, tone, and non-verbal cues, ensuring that their messages are conveyed accurately and with sensitivity. They actively listen to others, seeking to understand before responding, and promote open dialogue to foster better collaboration.

5. Collaboration and Shared Vision: Mindful entrepreneurs embrace collaboration as a means to achieve shared goals and a shared vision. They value diverse perspectives and actively seek out opportunities for collaboration, knowing that it leads to innovative solutions and collective growth. Mindful entrepreneurs create an inclusive and collaborative environment where all stakeholders feel valued and empowered to contribute their unique insights and skills.

6. Conflict Resolution and Relationship
   Maintenance: Conflicts are inevitable in
   any business relationship. Mindful
   entrepreneurs approach conflicts with a
   constructive mindset, seeking resolution
   through open communication, active
   listening, and a focus on finding
   mutually beneficial solutions. They
   prioritize the long-term health of the
   relationship over individual ego or
   short-term gains. Mindful entrepreneurs
   understand that conflict resolution is an
   opportunity for growth, improved
   understanding, and the strengthening of
   the bond between individuals or
   organizations.

By embracing mindfulness in their approach
to relationships, entrepreneurs can cultivate a
business environment that fosters
authenticity, effective communication,
collaboration, and empathy. Mindful
relationships not only enhance individual
well-being but also contribute to a positive
work culture, increased productivity, and the
long-term success of entrepreneurial ventures.

Chapter 5: Mindfulness in Decision-Making and Problem-Solving

Mindfulness is a valuable tool for entrepreneurs when it comes to making informed and conscious decisions, overcoming biases, enhancing critical thinking, approaching problems with a clear and focused mindset, and adapting to changing circumstances. By incorporating mindfulness into their decision-making and problem-solving processes, entrepreneurs can navigate the complexities of entrepreneurship with greater clarity, wisdom, and effectiveness.

Using Mindfulness to Make Informed and Conscious Decisions

Mindful entrepreneurs understand that decisions made in haste or without proper consideration can have significant consequences for their business. By practicing mindfulness, entrepreneurs can cultivate a state of heightened awareness and clarity, enabling them to make informed and conscious decisions. Mindfulness allows entrepreneurs to tap into their intuition, assess the available information, and consider the potential outcomes of their decisions. By approaching decision-making mindfully, entrepreneurs are more likely to align their choices with their values, long-term goals, and the best interests of their business.

Overcoming Biases and Enhancing Critical Thinking

Unconscious biases can cloud judgment and hinder effective decision-making. Mindful entrepreneurs are aware of these biases and actively work to overcome them. Through mindfulness practice, entrepreneurs develop the ability to observe their thoughts, emotions, and biases without judgment. This self-awareness allows them to identify and challenge their biases, enhancing their critical thinking skills. Mindful entrepreneurs are more open to alternative perspectives and more willing to consider diverse viewpoints, which leads to more well-rounded and balanced decision-making.

Approaching Problems with a Clear and Focused Mindset

Entrepreneurship often presents complex problems and challenges that require careful analysis and innovative solutions. Mindfulness helps entrepreneurs approach problems with a clear and focused mindset. By cultivating present-moment awareness, entrepreneurs can free their minds from distractions, past experiences, or future concerns that may hinder their ability to find creative solutions. Mindful entrepreneurs learn to observe their thoughts and emotions related to the problem at hand without becoming overwhelmed or attached to them. This non-reactive mindset allows for a more objective and balanced assessment of the situation, leading to more effective problem-solving.

Applying Mindfulness to Adapt to Changing Circumstances

In today's rapidly evolving business landscape, adaptability is key to entrepreneurial success. Mindful entrepreneurs leverage mindfulness to navigate change and uncertainty with resilience and flexibility. Mindfulness practice fosters an attitude of acceptance and non-attachment, allowing entrepreneurs to respond to unexpected circumstances with equanimity. Instead of resisting or becoming overwhelmed by change, mindful entrepreneurs embrace it as an opportunity for growth and learning. They adapt their strategies, pivot when necessary, and make agile decisions that align with the current business environment.

By integrating mindfulness into their decision-making and problem-solving processes, entrepreneurs can make more informed choices, overcome biases, enhance critical thinking, approach problems with clarity, and adapt to changing circumstances. Mindful entrepreneurs are better equipped to navigate the challenges and complexities of entrepreneurship, leading to greater success, innovation, and resilience in their business ventures.

Chapter 6:

Mindful Leadership and Ethical Entrepreneurship

Mindful leadership and ethical entrepreneurship go hand in hand, as they emphasize the importance of leading with integrity, promoting well-being, and creating a positive impact on society. By embracing mindful leadership principles and practices, entrepreneurs can foster a culture of ethical decision-making, balance success with well-being, promote social responsibility, and create a positive and inclusive work environment.

Mindful Leadership Principles and Practices

Mindful leaders embody qualities such as self-awareness, empathy, authenticity, and compassion. They lead by example, cultivating a culture of mindfulness and well-being within their organizations. Mindful leaders prioritize active listening and open communication, valuing the input and perspectives of their team members. They create a space where individuals feel safe to express themselves, fostering collaboration, innovation, and trust. Mindful leaders also empower their team members, encouraging personal and professional growth, and promoting a sense of purpose and fulfillment.

Balancing Success and Well-being in Entrepreneurial Ventures

Entrepreneurship often comes with long hours, high expectations, and relentless pursuit of success. However, mindful entrepreneurs understand the importance of balancing success with well-being. They recognize that a sustainable and fulfilling entrepreneurial journey requires attention to their physical, mental, and emotional well-being. Mindful entrepreneurs prioritize self-care, setting boundaries, and creating a healthy work-life balance. They encourage their team members to do the same, promoting a culture that values overall well-being and recognizes the importance of rest, self-reflection, and rejuvenation.

Promoting Social Responsibility and Ethical Business Practices

Ethical entrepreneurship goes beyond financial success and encompasses the impact a business has on its stakeholders and society at large. Mindful entrepreneurs are committed to conducting their business in an ethical and socially responsible manner. They consider the environmental, social, and economic implications of their decisions and actions. Mindful entrepreneurs promote fair and transparent business practices, treating their employees, customers, suppliers, and the community with respect and integrity. They strive to create positive social impact through their products, services, and philanthropic initiatives, aligning their business goals with the betterment of society.

Creating a Positive and Inclusive Work Culture through Mindfulness

A positive and inclusive work culture is essential for attracting and retaining talented individuals and fostering collaboration and innovation. Mindful entrepreneurs use mindfulness practices to create a supportive and inclusive work environment. They encourage open and honest communication, value diverse perspectives, and actively promote psychological safety. Mindful entrepreneurs prioritize cultivating a culture of gratitude, kindness, and appreciation, recognizing and celebrating the contributions of their team members. They also foster a sense of belonging, ensuring that every individual feels respected, valued, and included, regardless of their background or identity.

By embracing mindful leadership principles and ethical entrepreneurship, entrepreneurs can create organizations that prioritize well-being, social responsibility, and a positive work culture. Mindful leaders inspire their team members, foster collaboration and innovation, and create a lasting impact on society. Through their conscious and compassionate leadership, mindful entrepreneurs pave the way for a more sustainable, inclusive, and ethical business landscape.

Chapter 7:
The Mindful Entrepreneur's Toolkit

The Mindful Entrepreneur's Toolkit provides practical tools, exercises, and resources to support entrepreneurs in integrating mindfulness into their daily lives and business practices. This toolkit equips entrepreneurs with the necessary skills and knowledge to cultivate a mindful entrepreneurial mindset, enhance self-awareness, and achieve sustainable success. The toolkit includes:

Practical Mindfulness Exercises and Techniques

The toolkit offers a variety of mindfulness exercises and techniques specifically tailored for entrepreneurs. These exercises help entrepreneurs develop present-moment awareness, manage stress, improve focus and concentration, and cultivate emotional intelligence. Examples of exercises include mindful breathing, body scan meditation, mindful eating, and walking meditation. The toolkit provides step-by-step instructions, tips, and guidance to help entrepreneurs incorporate these exercises into their daily routines.

Incorporating Mindfulness into Daily Routines and Rituals

Mindfulness is most effective when integrated into daily routines and rituals. The toolkit offers guidance on how to infuse mindfulness into various aspects of an entrepreneur's day, such as morning routines, work breaks, and end-of-day reflections. It provides practical strategies for creating mindful transitions between tasks, setting intentions, and maintaining a sense of presence and focus throughout the day. Entrepreneurs will learn how to leverage everyday activities and moments as opportunities for mindfulness practice.

Resources for Continued Personal and Professional Growth

The journey of the mindful entrepreneur is one of continuous learning and growth. The toolkit provides a curated list of resources to support entrepreneurs in their personal and professional development. This includes recommended books, podcasts, online courses, and mindfulness apps that can deepen their understanding of mindfulness, entrepreneurship, leadership, and well-being. Entrepreneurs can explore these resources at their own pace and tailor their learning journey to their specific needs and interests.

Case Studies and Real-Life Examples of Mindful Entrepreneurship

To inspire and provide practical insights, the toolkit includes case studies and real-life examples of entrepreneurs who have successfully integrated mindfulness into their business ventures. These case studies highlight how mindfulness has influenced their decision-making, problem-solving, leadership styles, and overall business success. By examining these real-world examples, entrepreneurs can gain valuable perspectives and apply the principles of mindful entrepreneurship to their own endeavors.

The Mindful Entrepreneur's Toolkit is a comprehensive resource that empowers entrepreneurs to harness the transformative power of mindfulness. By incorporating practical exercises, integrating mindfulness into daily routines, offering resources for continued growth, and showcasing real-life examples, the toolkit supports entrepreneurs in developing the necessary skills, mindset, and practices for sustainable success in business and personal life. With the tools provided in this toolkit, entrepreneurs can navigate the entrepreneurial journey with greater resilience, clarity, and fulfillment.

Chapter 8: Conclusion

In this final section of "The Mindful Entrepreneur," readers are invited to take a moment to reflect on their personal journey through the book and to internalize the key insights and takeaways they have gained along the way. This moment of reflection serves as a powerful reminder of the transformative power of mindfulness in the entrepreneurial context.

As readers reflect on their journey through the book, they are encouraged to consider how mindfulness has already influenced their perspective on entrepreneurship. They may recognize shifts in their awareness, a deeper understanding of their values and motivations, and an increased sense of clarity and purpose. By internalizing the key insights and takeaways, readers can anchor these valuable lessons within themselves, making them a part of their entrepreneurial mindset and approach.

The invitation to embark on a mindful entrepreneurial journey is an important call to action. It recognizes that reading about mindfulness and its benefits is just the beginning. True growth and transformation come from personal experience and practice. Encouraging readers to take their newfound knowledge and apply it to their own lives and businesses is where the real magic happens.

The encouragement to embark on a mindful entrepreneurial journey is a reminder that incorporating mindfulness into entrepreneurship is not just a nice-to-have, but a powerful tool for personal and professional growth. It is an invitation to embrace mindfulness as an integral part of their entrepreneurial toolkit, recognizing its potential to bring about profound changes in their approach to business, leadership, and well-being.

Moreover, the final thoughts in this section highlight the broader significance of mindfulness beyond the entrepreneurial realm. They remind readers that the transformative power of mindfulness extends beyond business success and permeates into every aspect of their lives. By cultivating mindfulness, individuals can experience greater overall well-being, improved relationships, and a deeper sense of fulfillment.

The potential for mindfulness to create a positive impact in both business and personal life is emphasized as a final thought. The book acknowledges that when entrepreneurs cultivate mindfulness, they not only benefit themselves but also have the potential to positively influence their teams, stakeholders, and the wider community. Mindful entrepreneurship can contribute to a more compassionate, conscious, and sustainable world.

In conclusion, "The Mindful Entrepreneur" invites readers to reflect on their journey, internalize the key insights, and embrace mindfulness as they embark on their own entrepreneurial path. It emphasizes the transformative power of mindfulness, encourages readers to apply what they have learned, and highlights the potential for mindfulness to create a positive impact in both business and personal life. By incorporating mindfulness into their entrepreneurial endeavors, readers have the opportunity to not only achieve success but also cultivate well-being, fulfillment, and a lasting positive influence.